Lighthouse Coloring Book For Adults

This Lighthouses Coloring book belongs to:

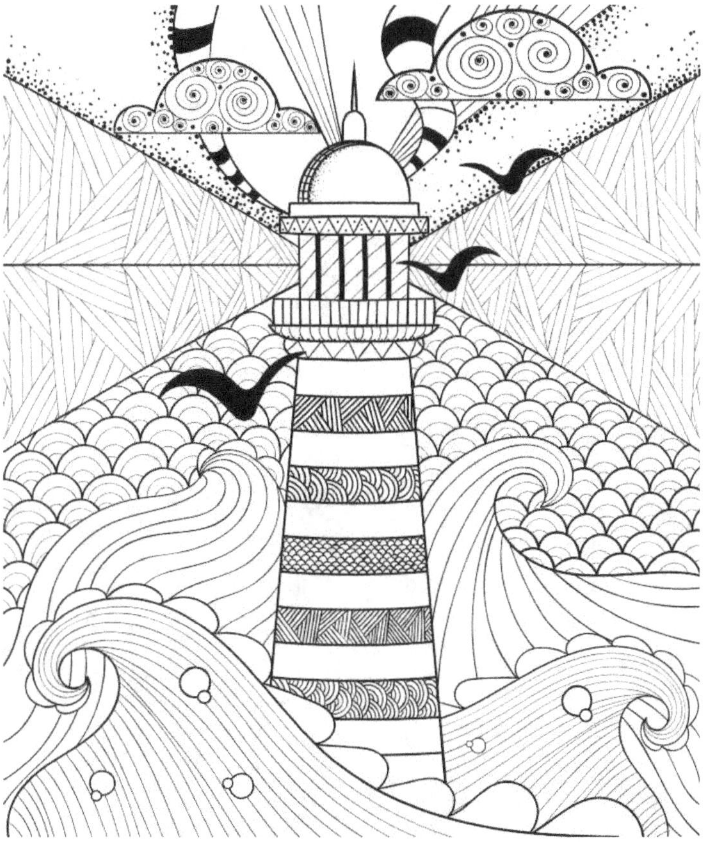

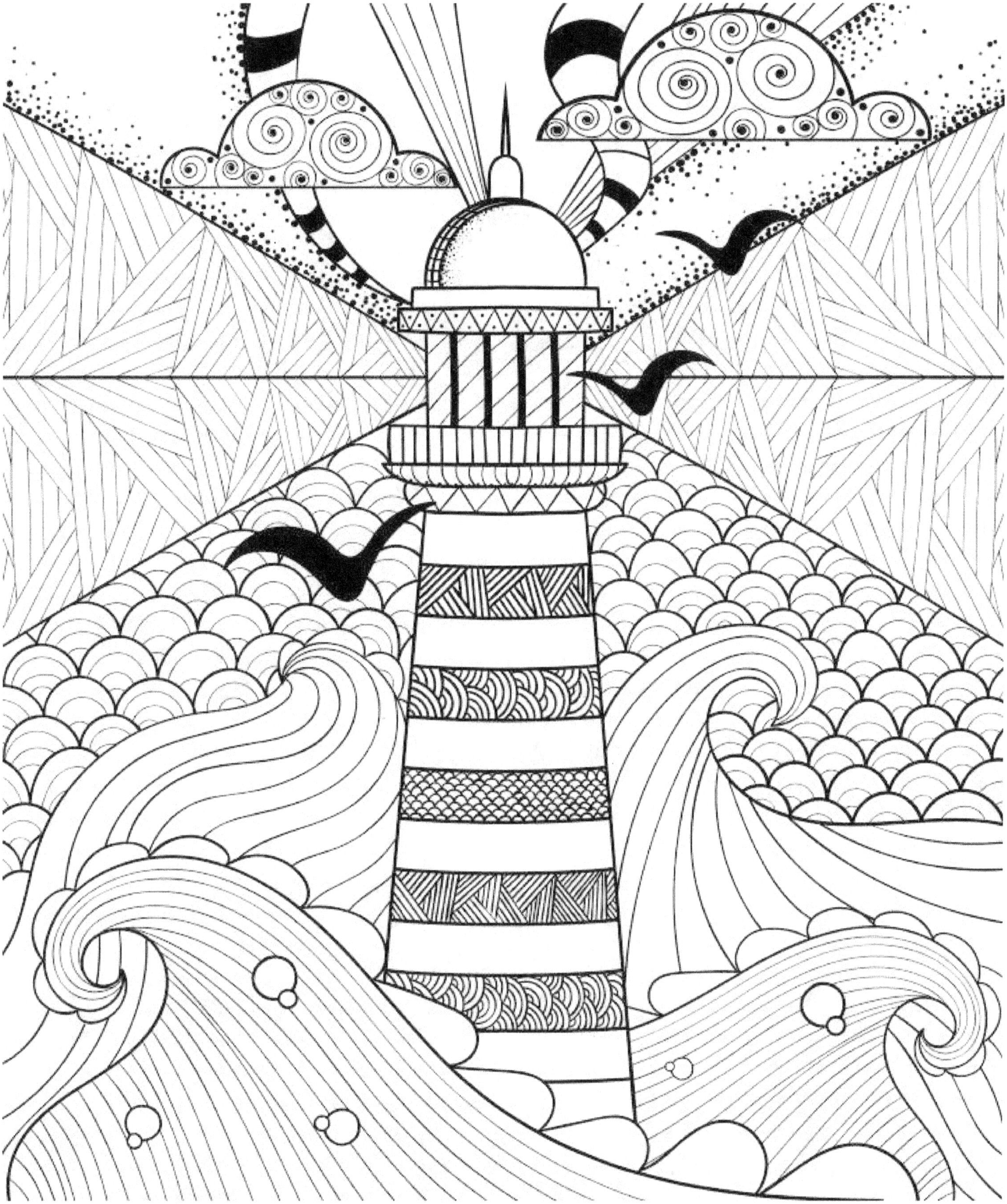

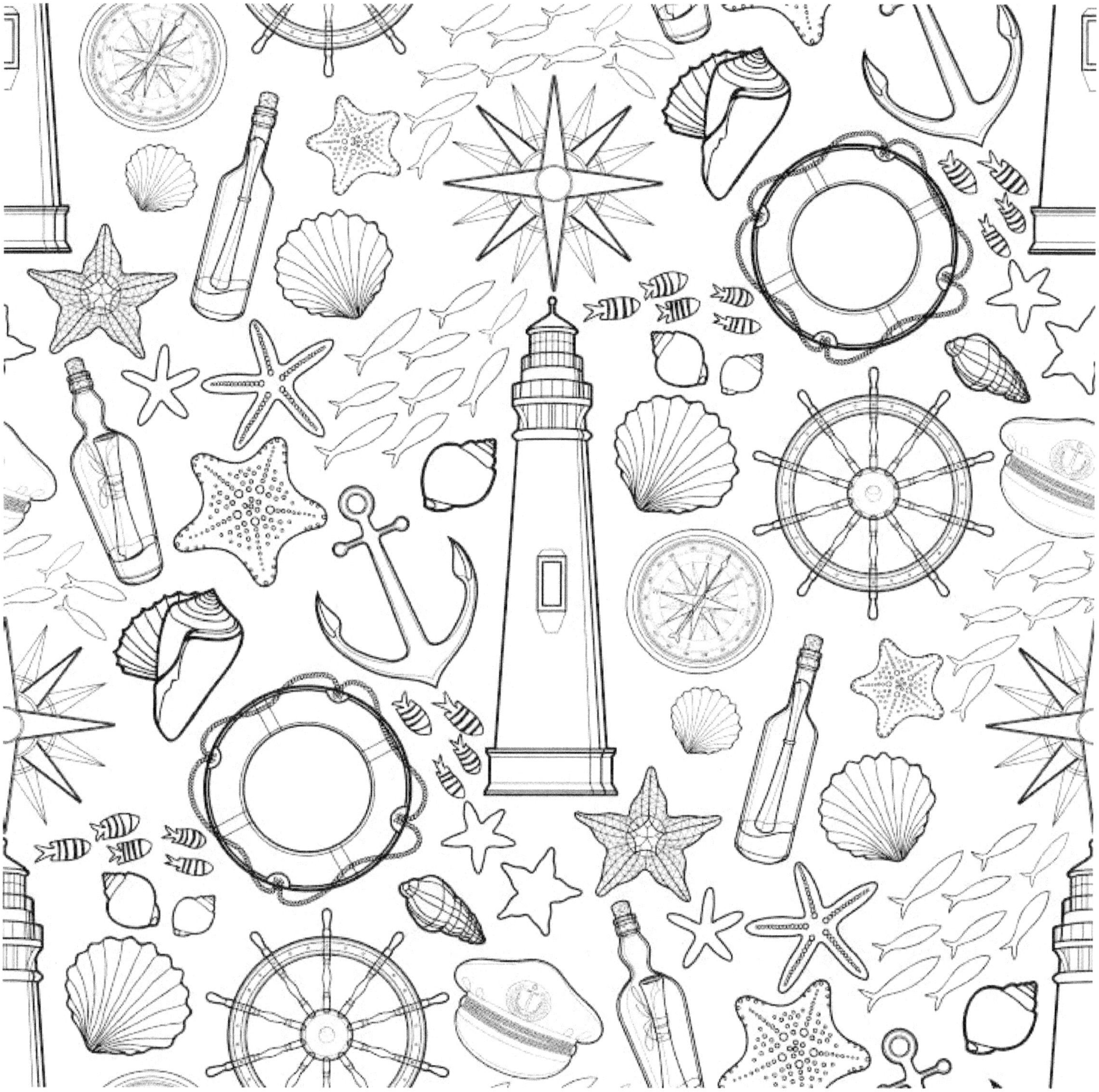

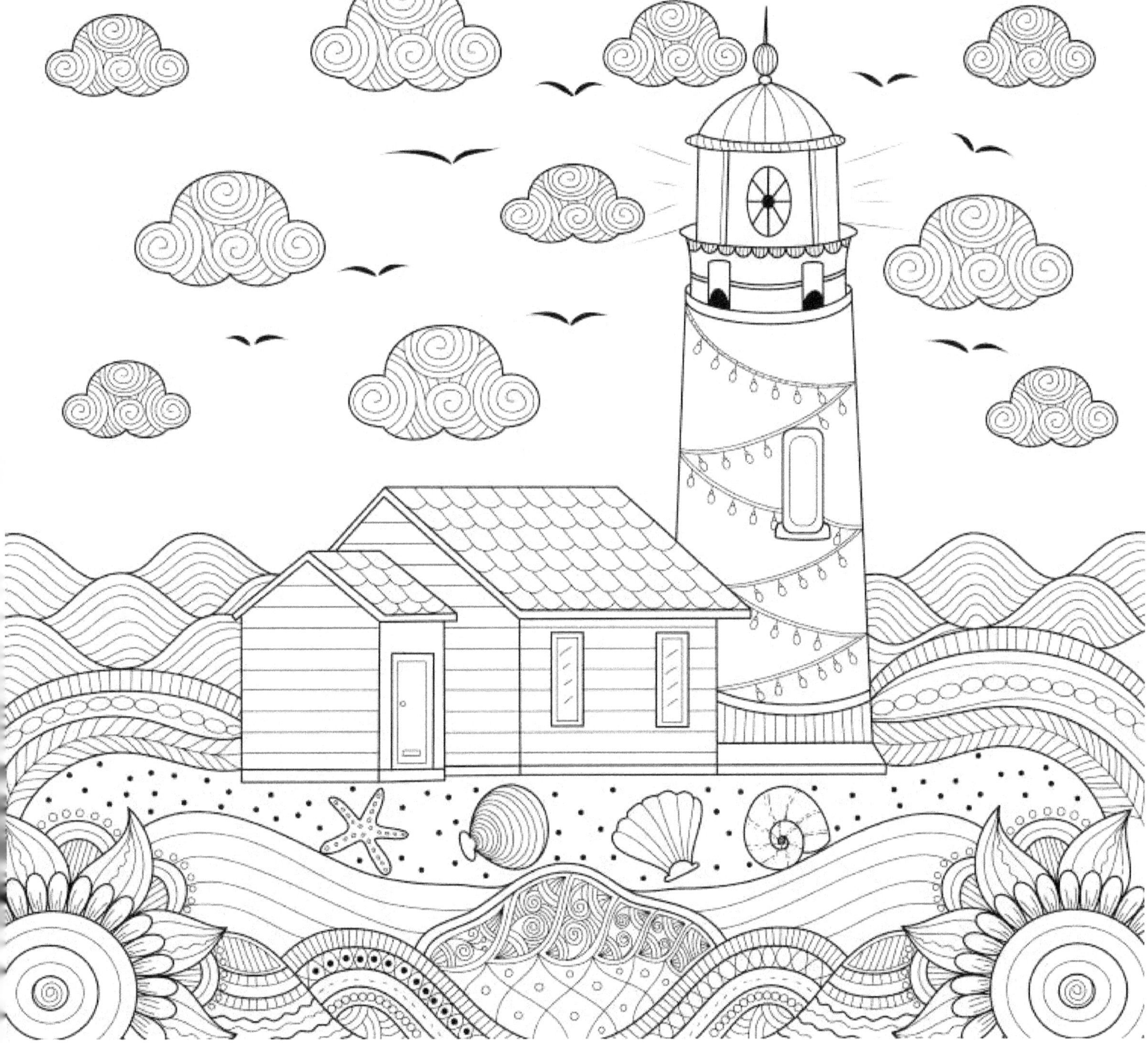

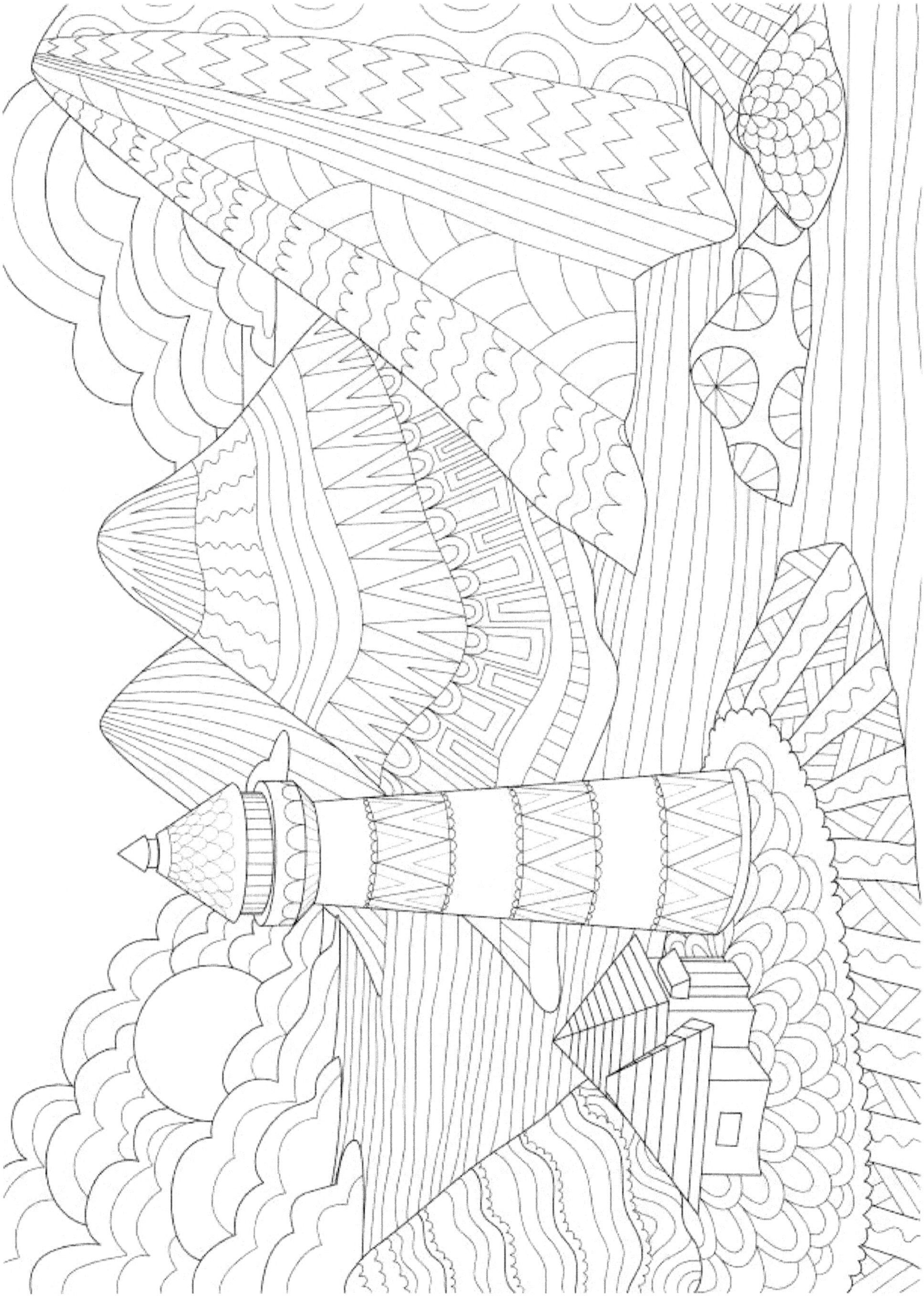

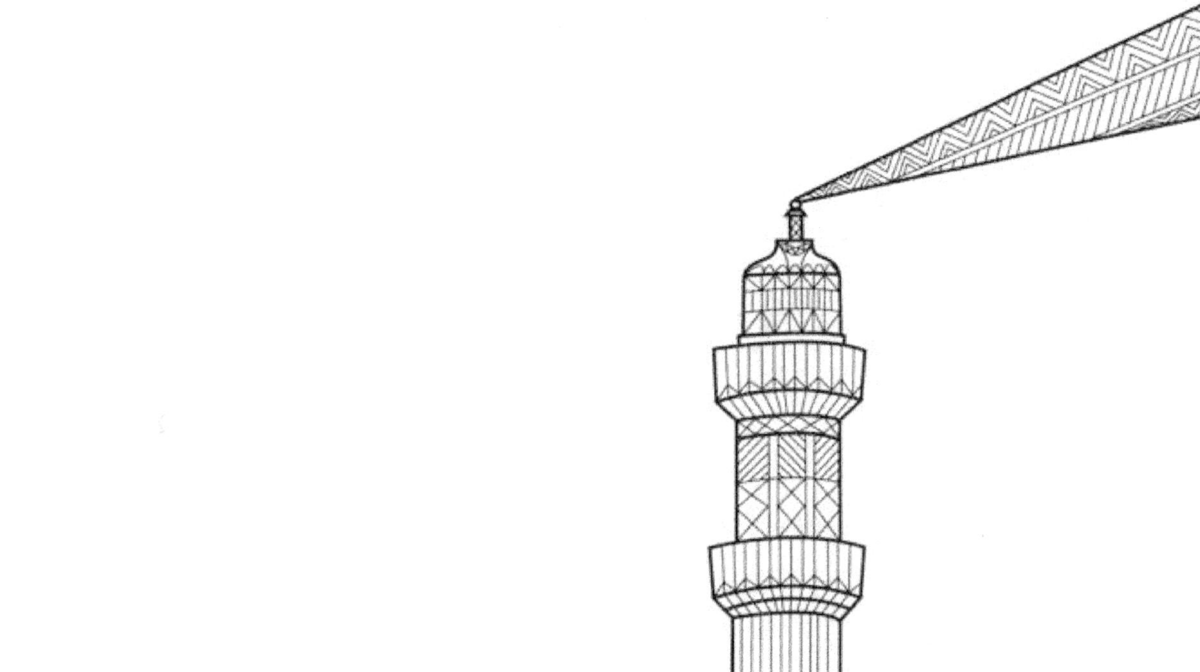

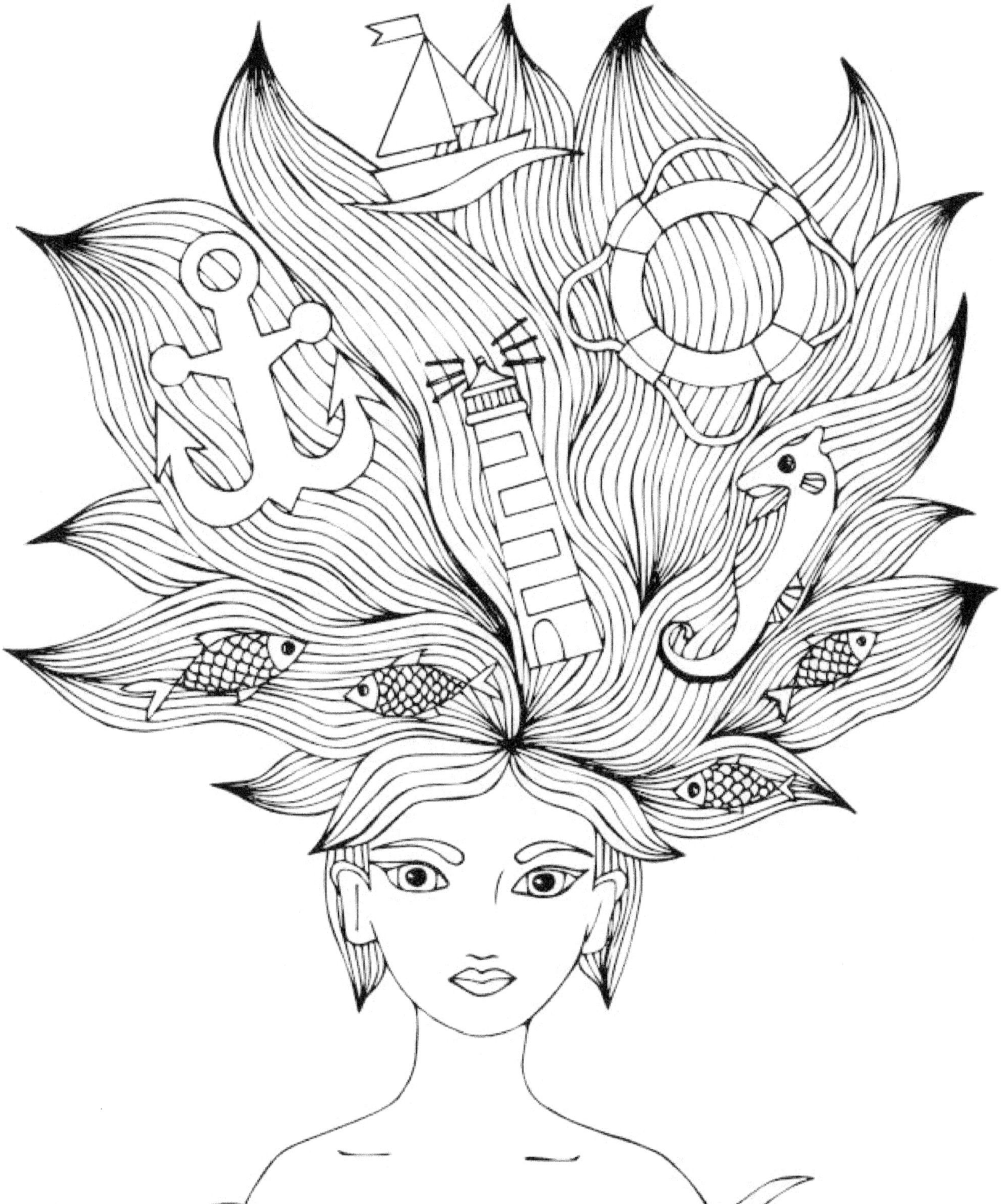

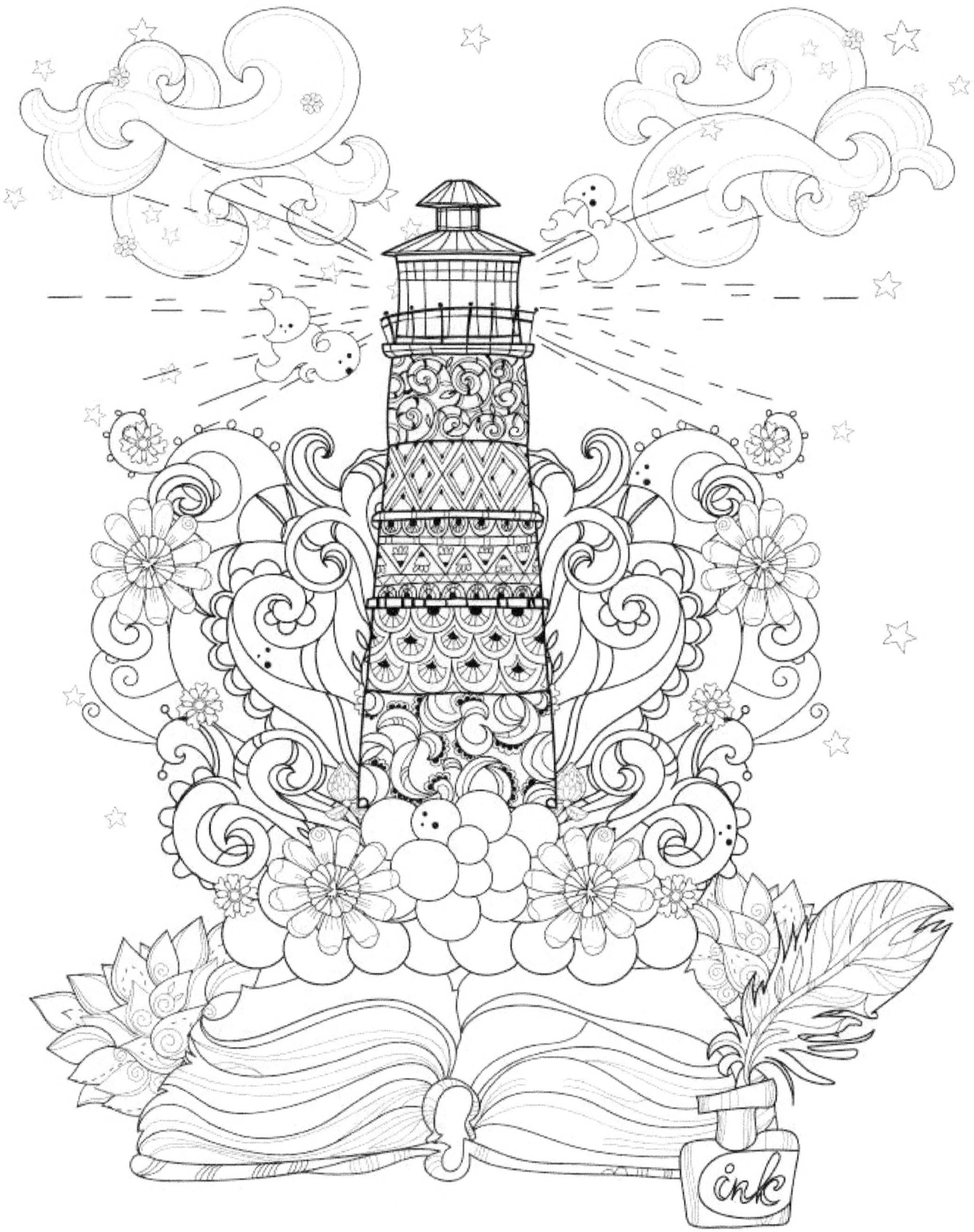
ink

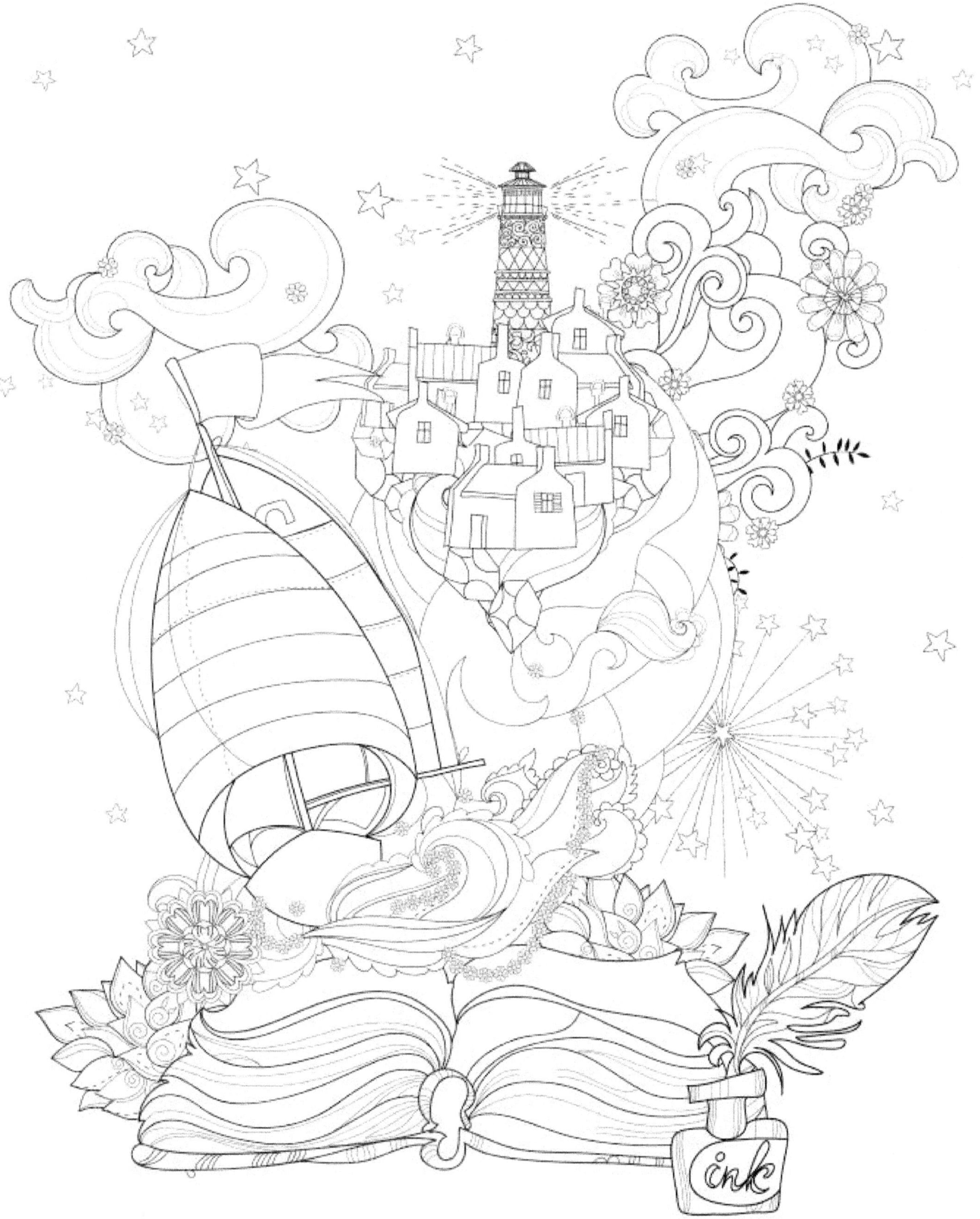
ink

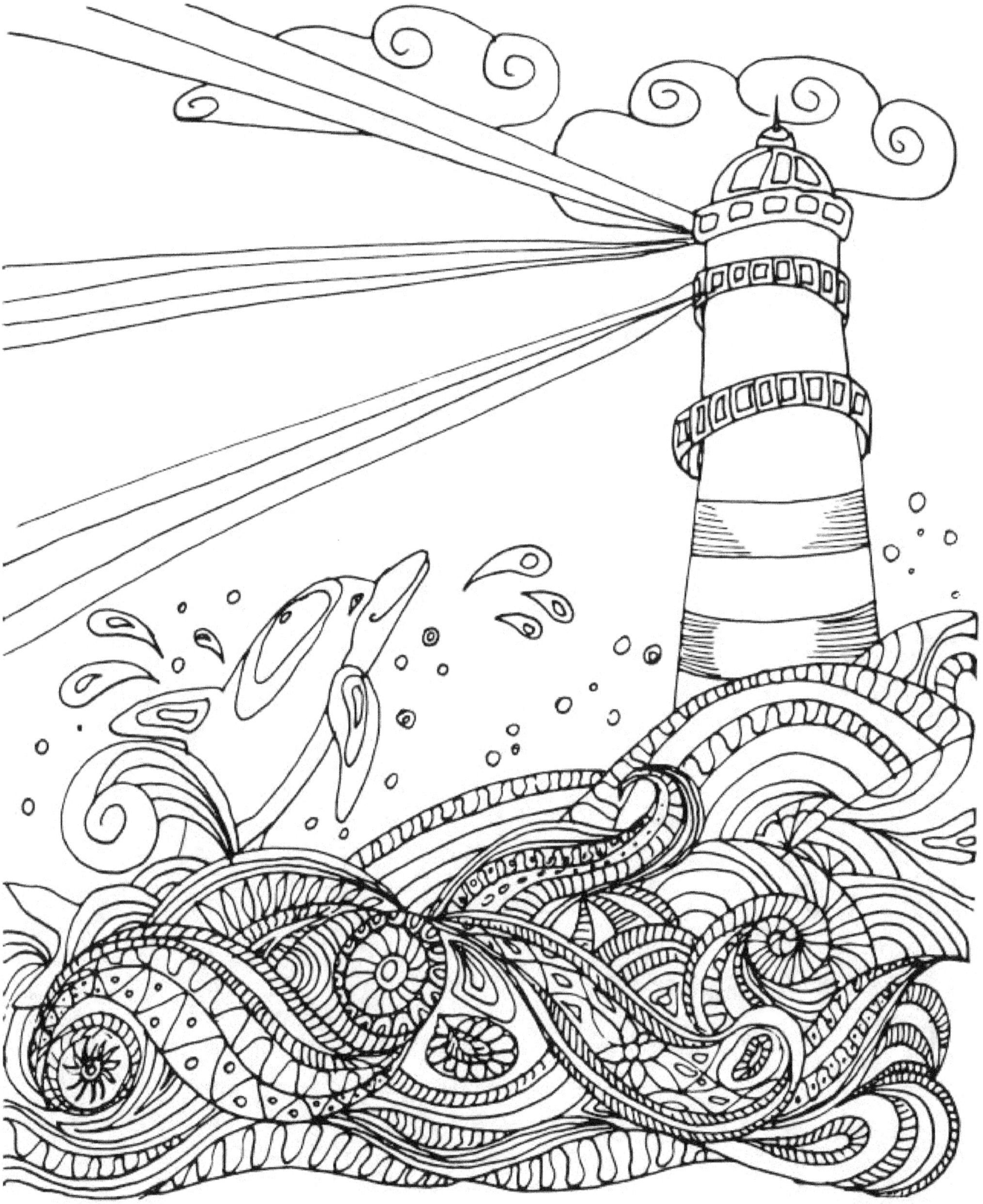

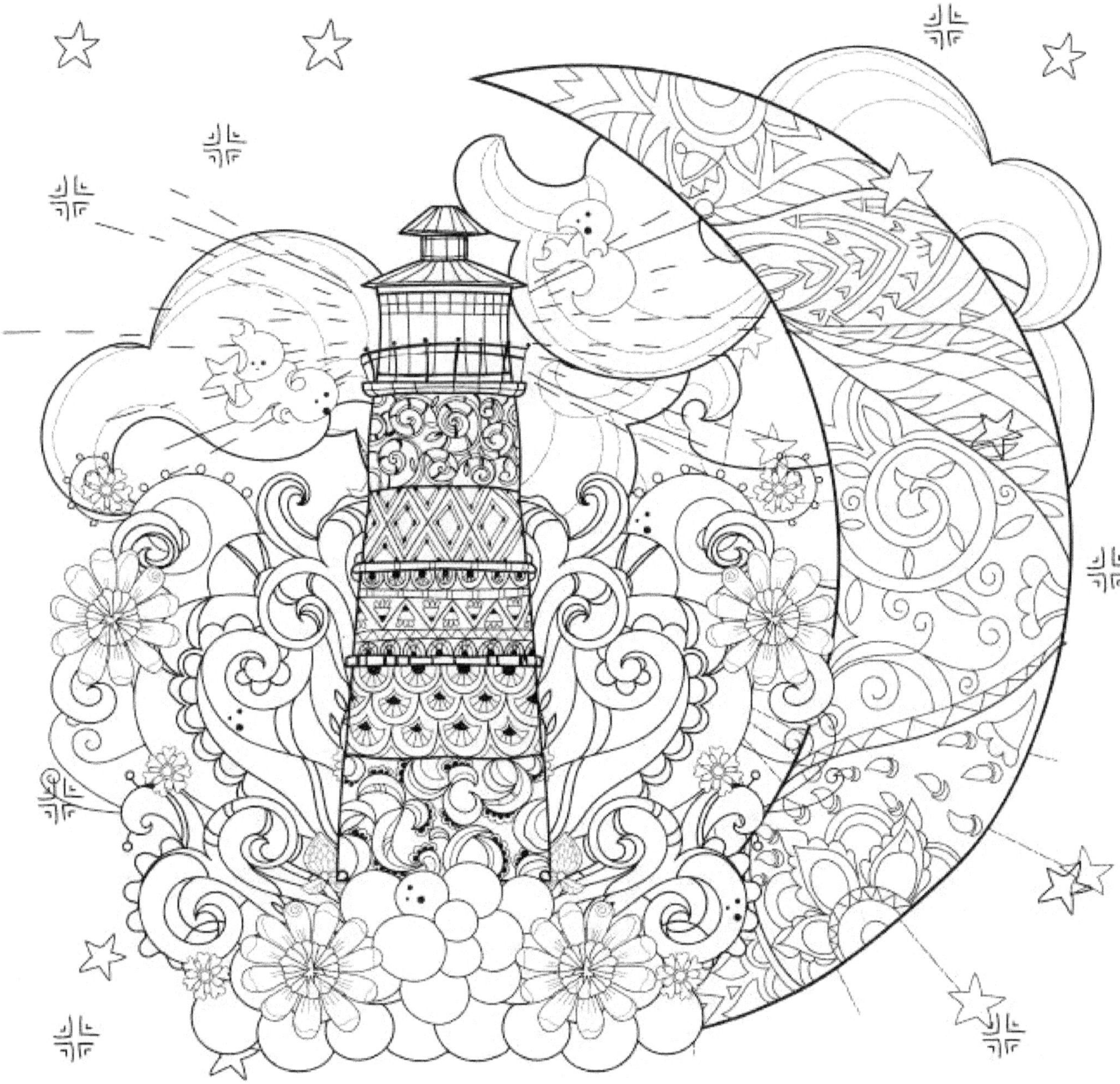

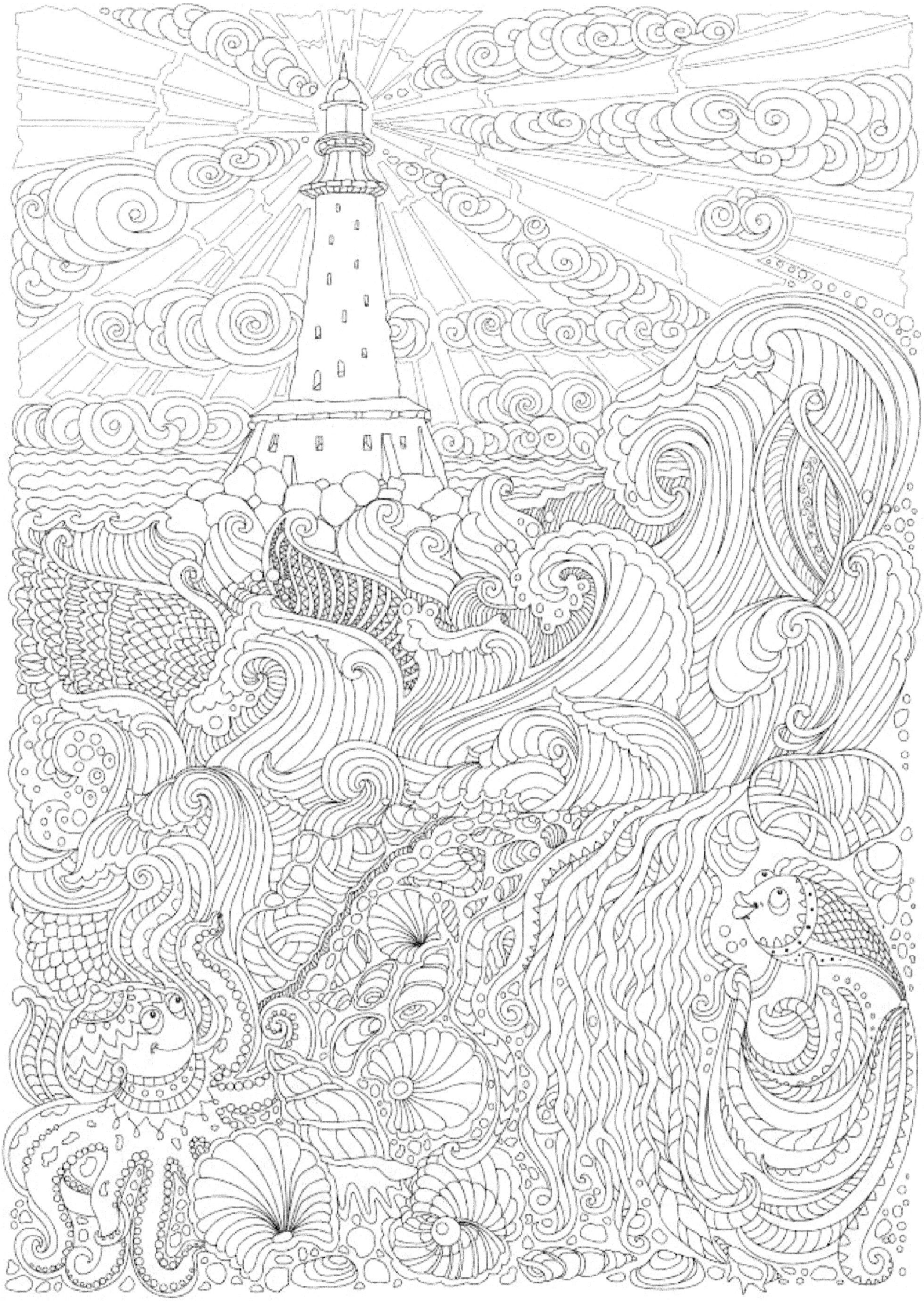

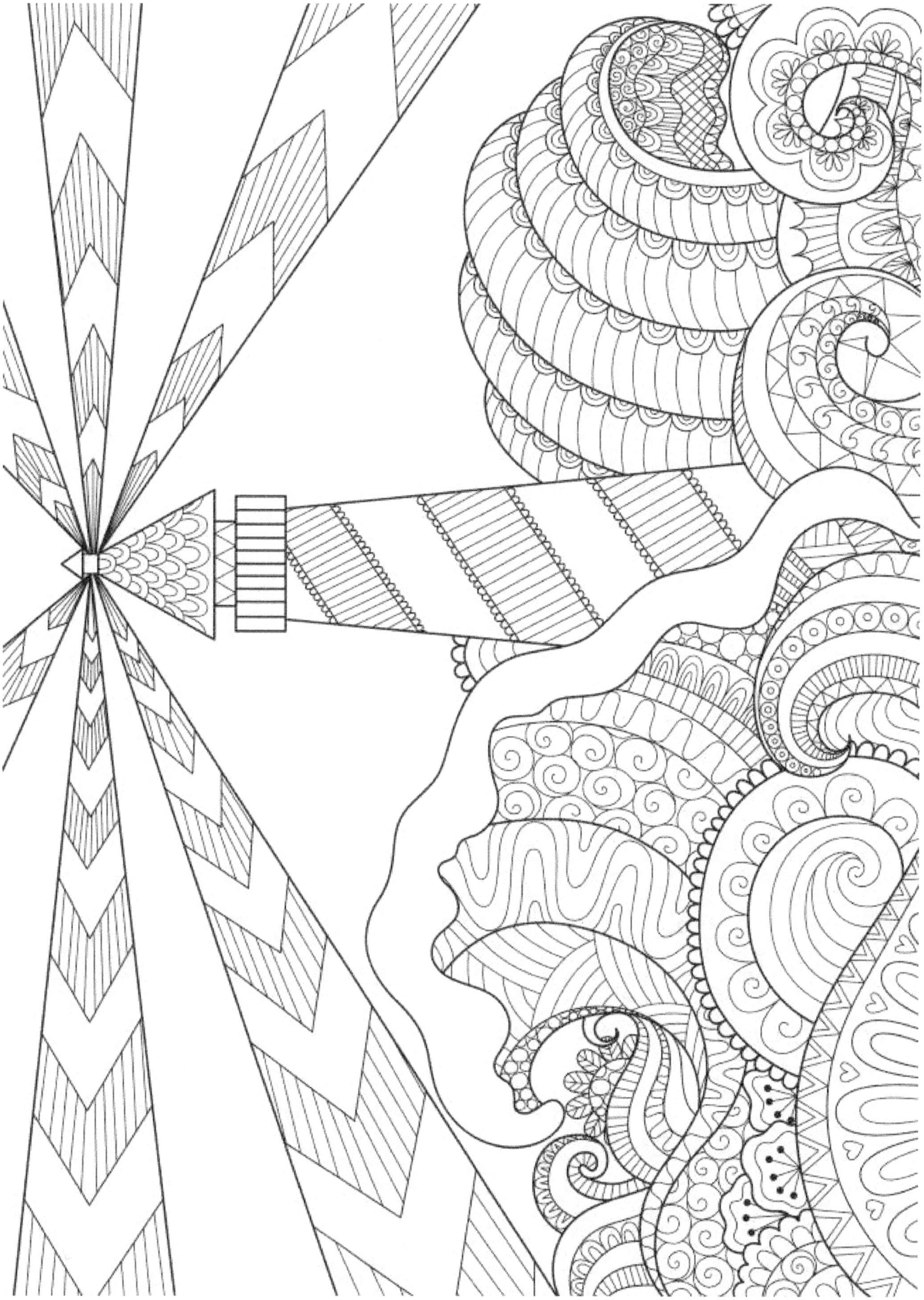

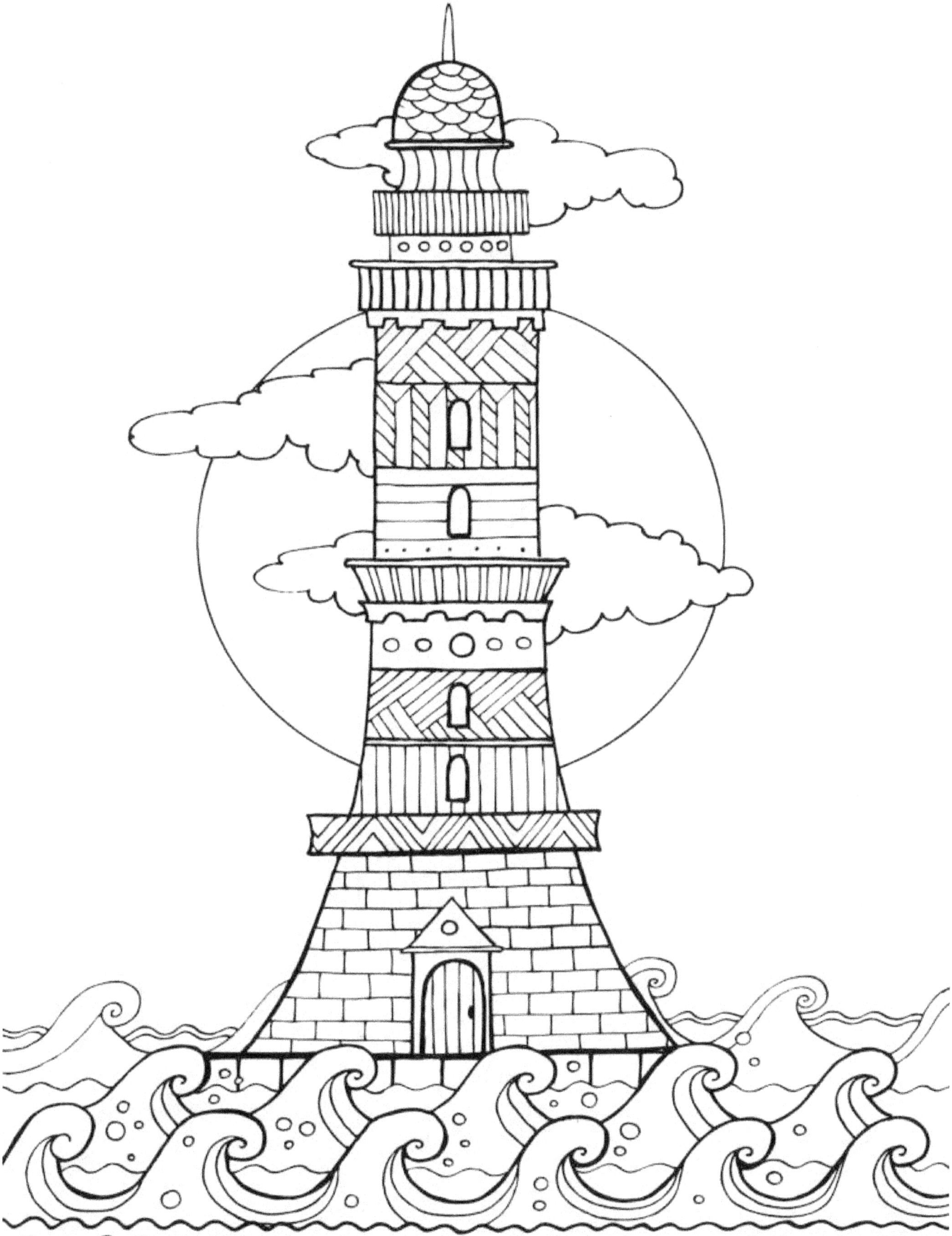

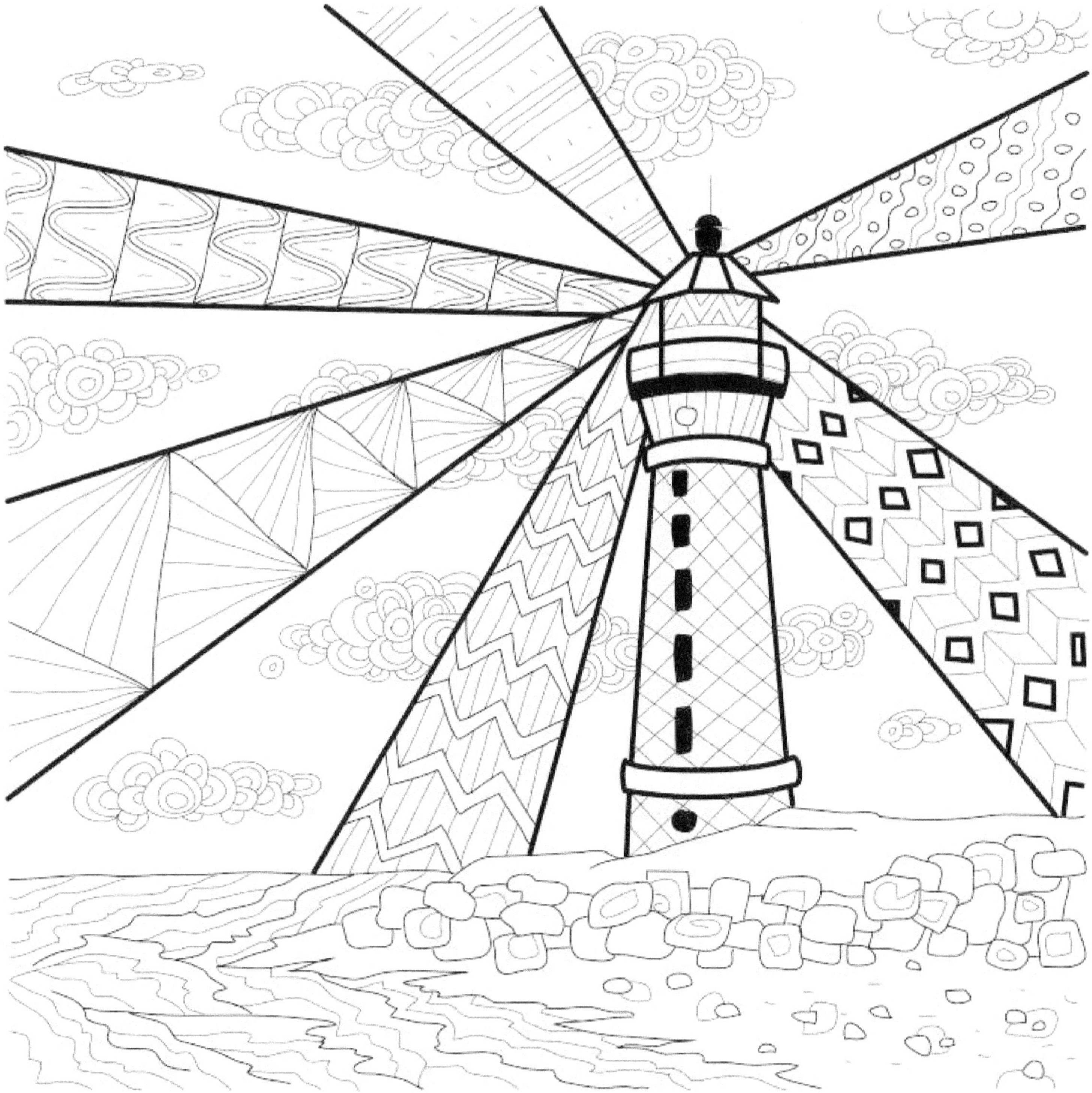

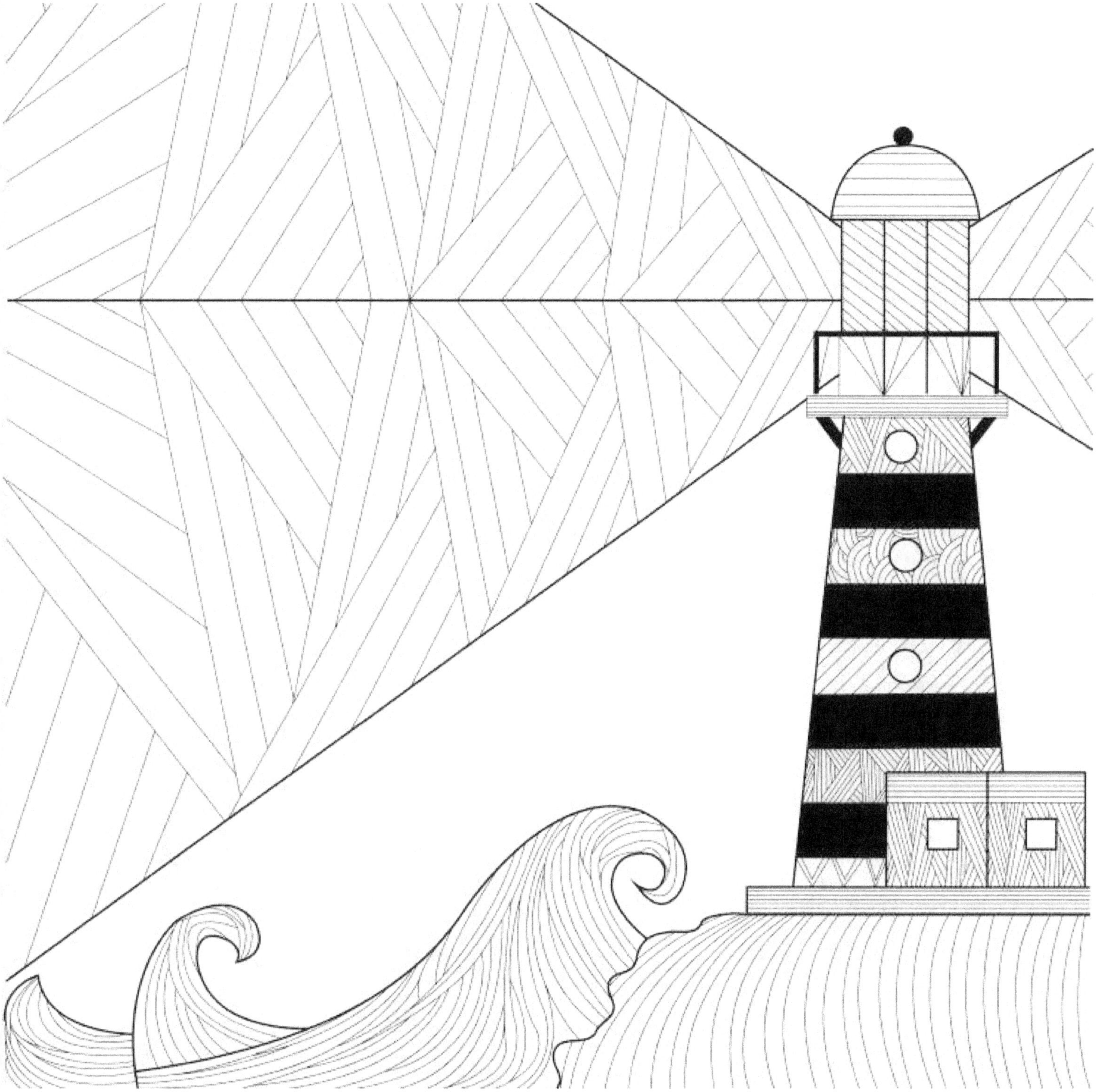

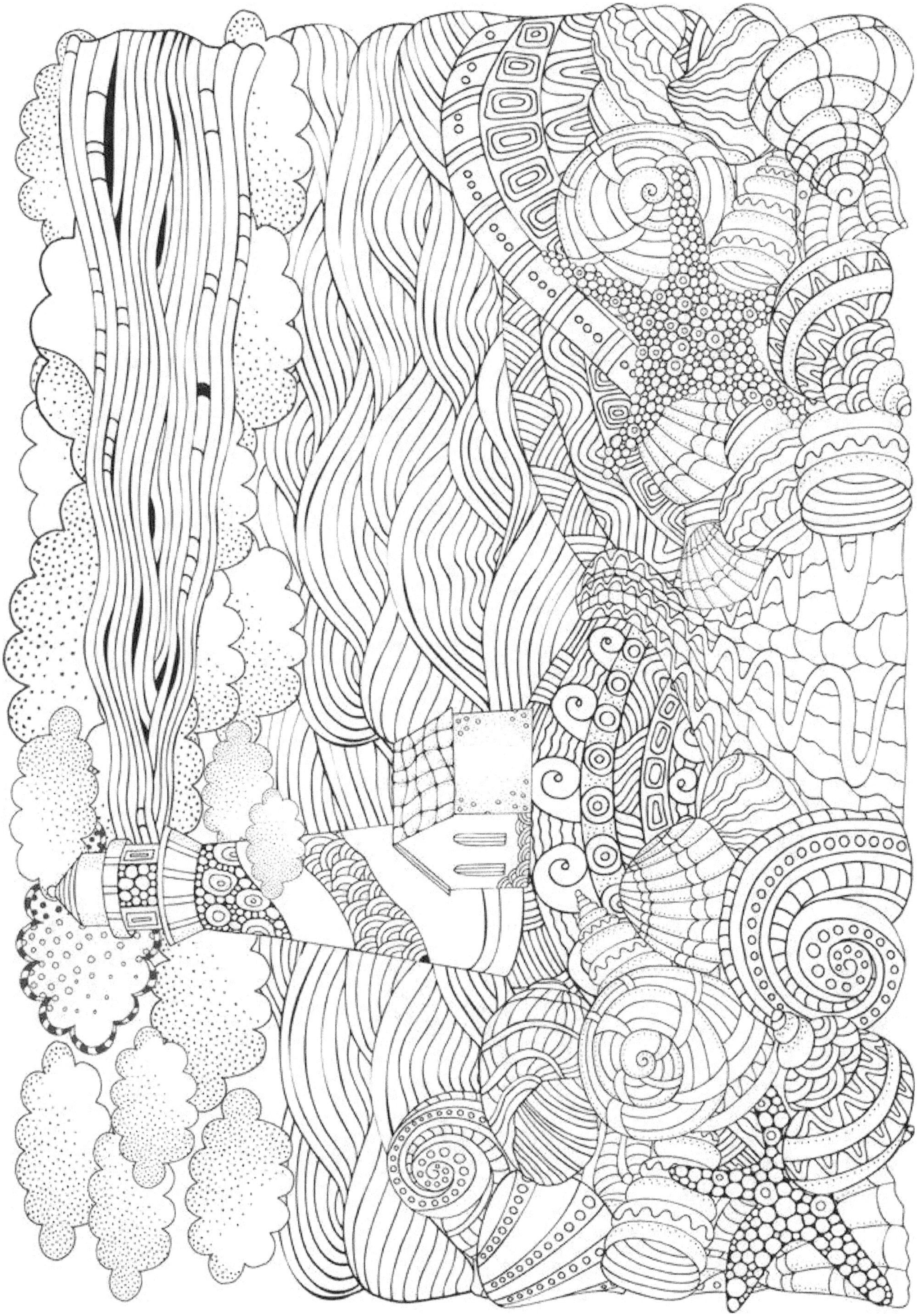

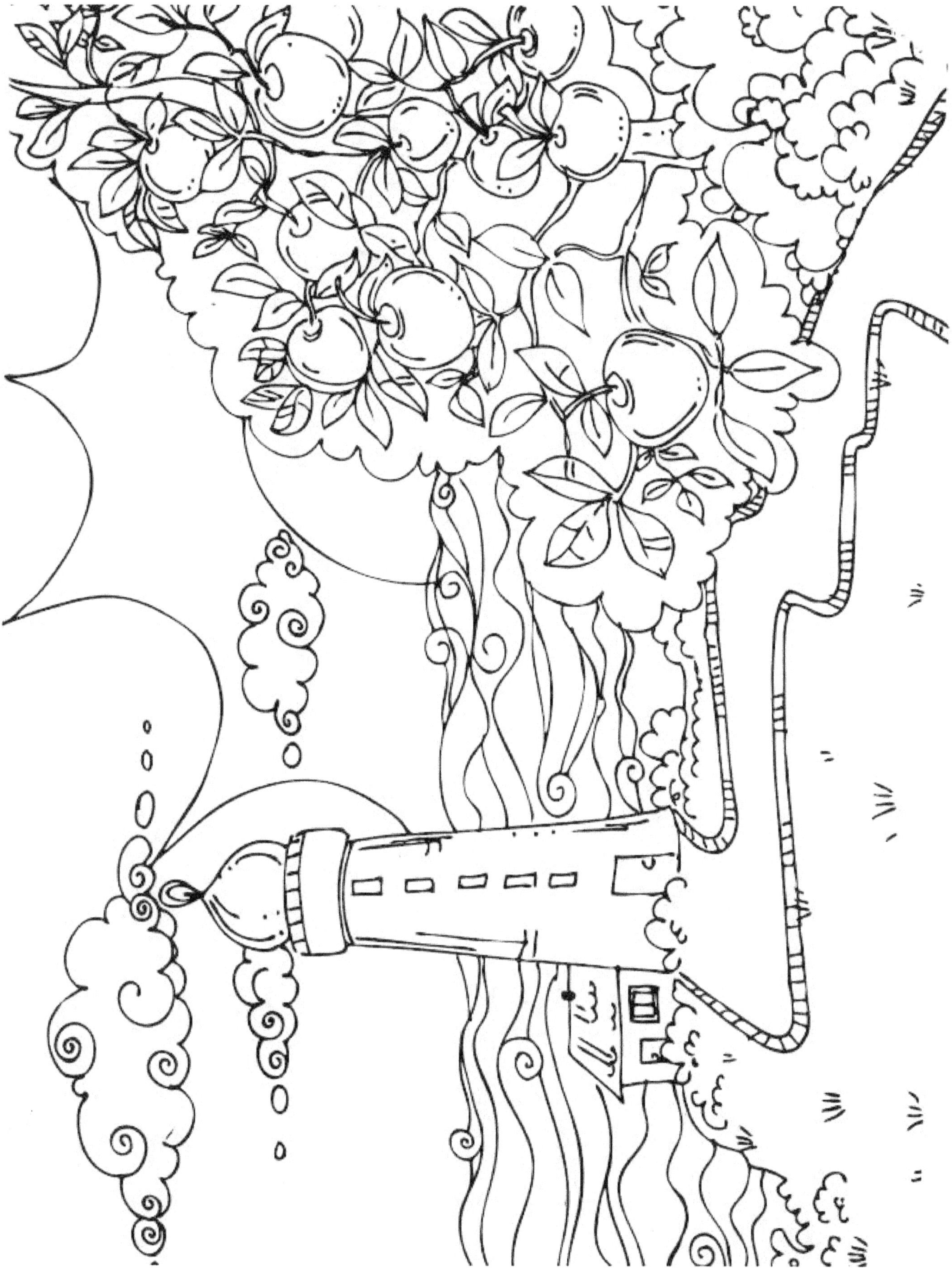

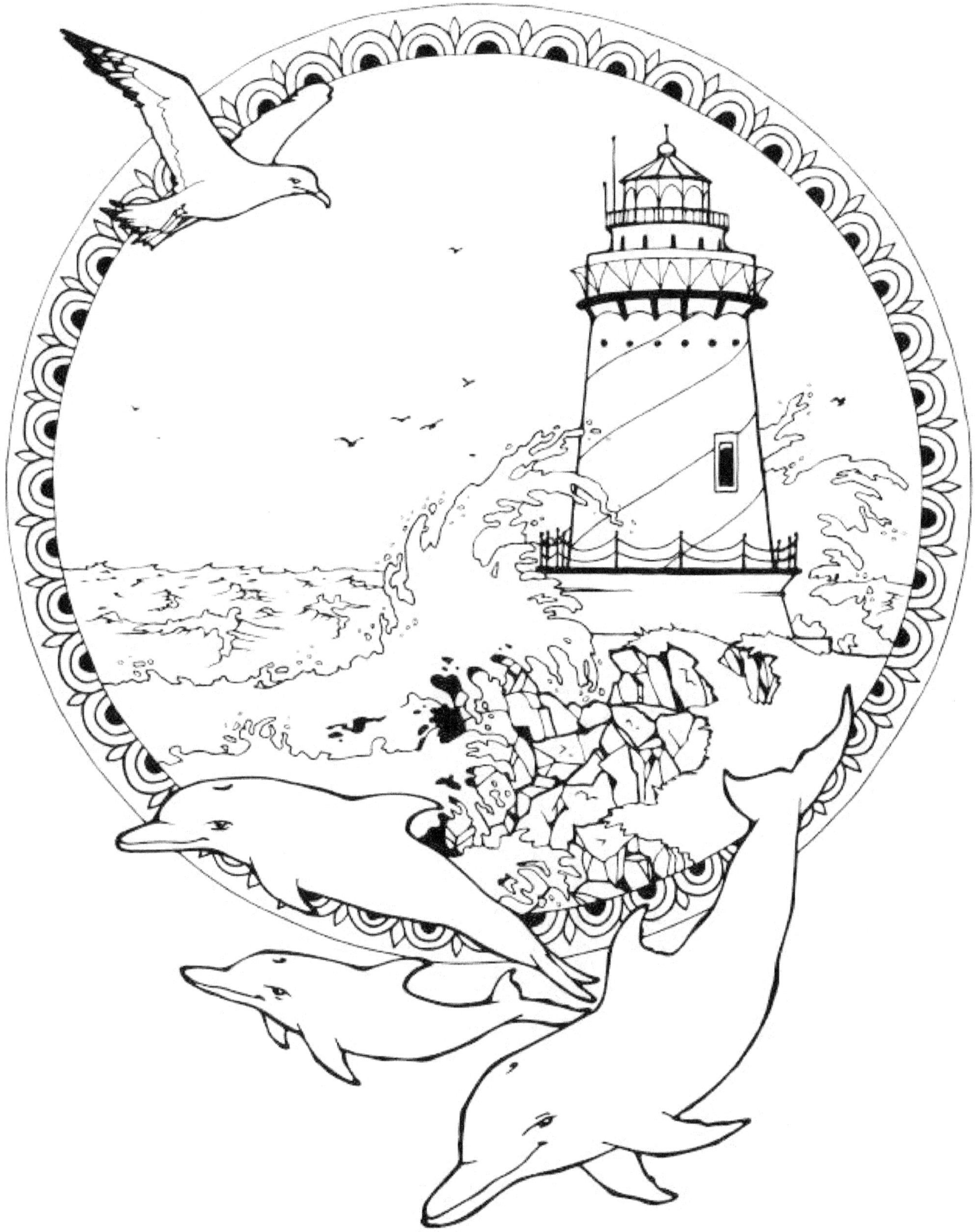

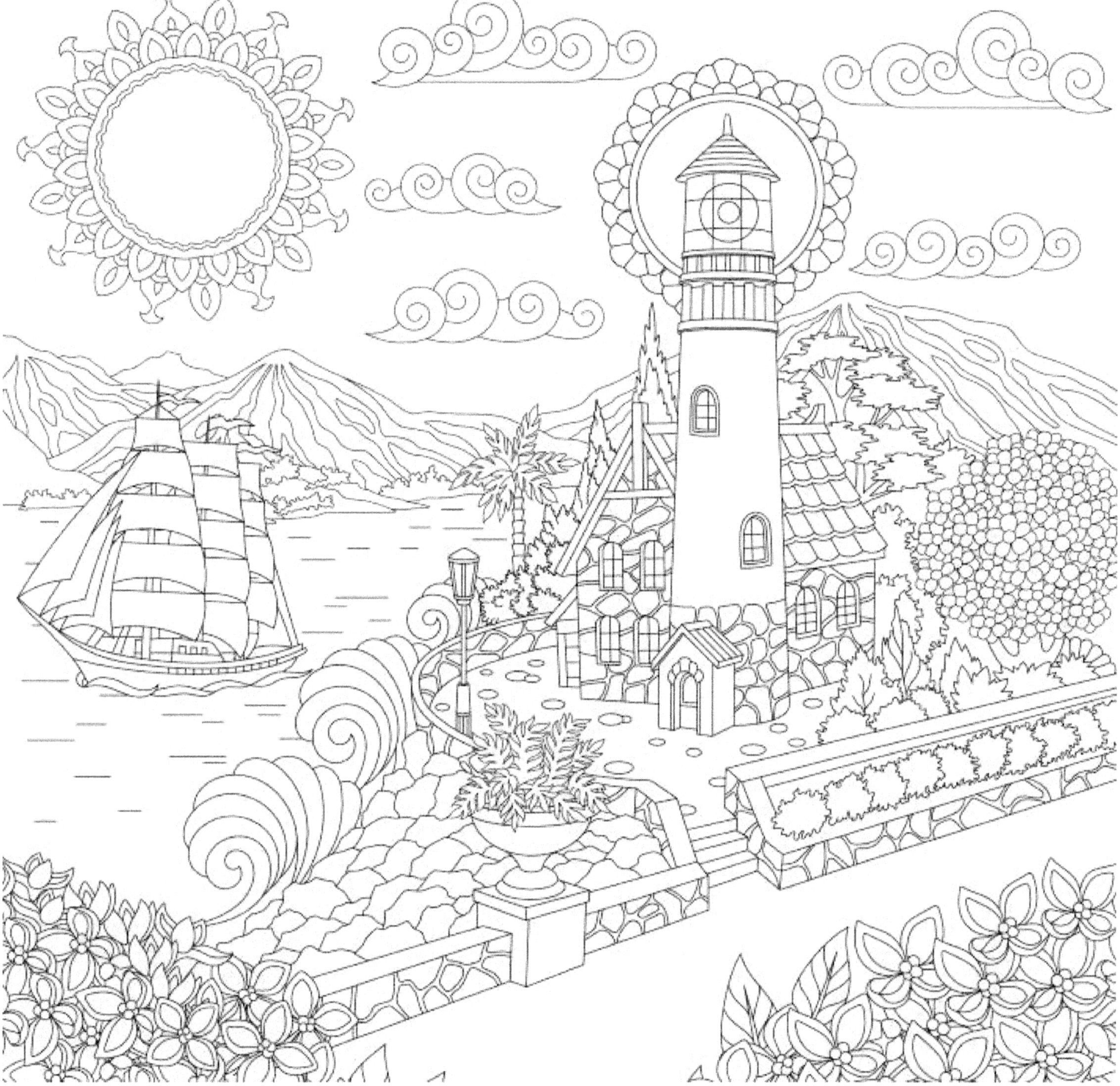

www.ingramcontent.com/pod-product-compliance
Lightning Source LLC
Chambersburg PA
CBHW081023170526
45158CB00010B/3140
9781096960317